YOU CAN BE LIKE JESUS

ADE SOBANJO

YOU CAN BE LIKE JESUS

FOUNDATIONAL STEPS TO STEADY GROWTH ON YOUR CHRISTIAN JOURNEY

AFROPAGES, KINGSTON, ONTARIO.

YOU CAN BE LIKE JESUS: Foundational Steps to Steady Growth on
Your Christian Journey
ISBN: 0-9781595-0-0
© 2011 by Ade Sobanjo

Published by Afropages
Kingston, Ontario. Canada.

Scriptural references are from:
NKJV - New King Jeames Version, 1982, Thomas Nelson, Inc
NET - New English Translation, 2004,2005 Biblical Studies Foundation.
NLT - New Living Translation, 2004 by Tyndale House Publishers, Inc.
NIV - New International Version, 1973, 1978, 1984 by International Bible
Society.

Contact:
Ade Sobanjo
ade@adesobanjo.org
1-800-948-7464

Printed in USA.

Contents

PREFACE

Can we really be like Jesus? Yes we can and that is what we are called to be. Every follower of Jesus is called by God to become like Jesus. Since Jesus was our perfect example, we have this confidence that God who made Jesus our example is able to make us to become like Him. This booklet started out as an attempt to write down a few pointers for those who want to develop their relationship with Christ. It has turned out in this format as a result of encouragement from several people notable amongst who is my precious wife and co-labourer Oluwaseun. Without her constant support, this booklet would still be in my head and my mouth.

My sincere thanks to my dear sister Dr Omobola Sobanjo who spent numerous hours reading and editing the manuscript. Thanks also to my father and mentor Dr Adebola Olubanjo for his constant support and to my mum Kenny Olubanjo whose gentle reminders kept this project on my mind. I thank the entire members of the Overcomers Assembly family who have inspired and encouraged me to be all that God wants me to be. Most importantly I thank God for the grace and privilege to write.

I pray that you dear readers will find blessings in the thoughts and insights expressed in this booklet.

Ade Sobanjo

Are you born again? Can you see the Kingdom of God?

"....The change is radical; it gives us new natures, makes us love what we hated and hate what we loved, sets us in a new road; makes our habits different, our thoughts different, makes us different in private, and different in public. So that being in Christ it is fulfilled: "If any man be in Christ he is a new creature; old things are passed away, behold all things are become new." - C.H. Spurgeon

Conversation....
God: *"Would you say that a person who watches 20 minutes of television a week worships the TV?"*
Us: *"Probably not."*
God: *"Then why would you say that someone who visits ME 20 minutes a week is a worshipper of God?"*
- Unknown.

INTRODUCTION

WHAT DOES IT MEAN
TO BE A CHRISTIAN?

*Jesus answered and said to him, "Most
assuredly, I say to you, unless one is born
again, he cannot see the kingdom of God."
(John 3:3 NKJV)*

*For with the heart one believes unto righ-
teousness, and with the mouth confession is
made unto salvation.
(Rom 10:10 NKJV)*

Becoming a Christian is the most important decision that anyone can make in life. When you say you
are a Christian, what does it mean? It means that you
have become aware of the love of God and the wretch-
edness of your previous life. As a result, you have de-
cided to stop living a selfish, self centered life; you have
now chosen to live the rest of your life to please God. It
means that you have asked God to forgive your sins and
are determined with the help of God, to run away from
all known sin because you have accepted the sacrifice

that was made on the cross by Jesus Christ on your be-half. Lastly, it means that you have begun a relationship with God the creator of the universe through Jesus Christ his son; as such you have received a new life.

Becoming a Christian is very much like being born as a child into this world. In fact Jesus describes it in John 3:3 as being born again. The apostle Peter ad-monishes new believers to desire the sincere milk of the word as new born babes (1 Peter 2:2). This outlines the need for anyone who wants to grow in Christ as a believ-er, to do certain things to ensure his/her growth. Just as no parent would dream of abandoning a child expecting it to grow automatically; it is very unrealistic to assume that when a person begins a relationship with Christ, they would simply grow automatically. NO! Every new Christian must be cared for and nurtured in the spirit so they can grow into mature Christians who in turn will be able to promote the work of our Lord Jesus on the earth and help others grow. More so, it is important to note that, if a person is truly "born again", that person will have a desire to know more about God, he or she will also want to talk to God and fellowship with other chil-dren of God.

Therefore, if you are reading this booklet and you discover that you do not have a desire to know more about God, Jesus or the Holy Spirit and you are not re-ally interested in fellowshipping with other Christians, then I must ask you firstly to get born-again or to renew your commitment to Christ. *A lack of spiritual hunger or thirst is a sign of serious spiritual sickness or lack of spiritual life.* The only way to develop an appetite for the things of God is REPENTANCE. This means a complete confession (first to God) of one's sins and a heartfelt desire and determination to leave those sins and turn to God. Simply put, it is a complete surrender of one's life to God to do with it what He created you for. For a detailed explanation of how to become a Christian please request for my tract on – "How to receive a brand new life".

 This booklet is written as an answer to a question that I have been asked over and over again as a pastor. From my mini-survey, I realized that one out of every 2 professing Christians wants to know how to grow in their faith. In this booklet, I present some basic steps that new believers can take to ensure continuous and fruitful development in their Christian walk. Although there are some practical steps suggested in this booklet, it is my belief that once a person comes into the right knowledge, it will trigger a corresponding action and as such, it is my prayer that as you read this booklet, you will discover some things that will help you move forward in your walk with God. This booklet will not and is not intended to replace the Bible; rather my aim with this booklet is to start you on a lifelong fruitful and exciting journey with God. You find in it a few basic things that every Christian needs to know for proper development as a Christian. If you practice these things and if they become a habit, you will grow and become a Christian who is able to help other Christians and bring those who do not know Christ into a relationship with Christ. Please note that if you have not begun a relationship with God through Jesus Christ, following these steps will only lead to frustration. Before arriving at the thought of growing as a Christian, you must be able to say yes to these 2 questions:

- Have you repented of your sins and surrendered your life to God?
- Have you received forgiveness of your sins through Christ Jesus?

An understanding of what it means to be "born again" is the starting point to growing as a Christian. As I have been growing as a Christian for over 20 years now, I have come to realize that the quest to fully grasp what it means to be born again as stated in John 3:3 or saved in Romans 10:10 is a life long quest. However, I have also discovered that for one to make any progress in developing a steady relationship with God, one must understand three things.

To be Christian is to be:
1) totally surrendered to God's will.
2) totally committed to God's plan
3) completely assured of God's ability to make us like Him (like Jesus); always motivated by love as opposed to selfishness.

If all you have done before now is to accept the Lord Jesus Christ as your saviour, I encourage you to also accept him as your Lord. Speak to God in your own words, be very deliberate and aware of each statement you make. God has a plan for you. Here is a sample prayer:

> *Dear Father, I thank you for saving me from sin and the consequences of my sins. I thank you for granting me your pardon through the work of Jesus Christ on the cross. From today, I surrender my will, my ambitions and my entire life to you. Do what ever you want with me. I trust your love and judgement. In Jesus Name.*

*A baptism of holiness, a demonstration of
godly living is the crying need of our day*
- Duncan Campbell

*This, and this alone, is Christianity, a uni-
versal holiness in every part of life, a heavenly wisdom in all our actions, not conform-
ing to the spirit and temper of the world but
turning all worldly enjoyments into means of
piety and devotion to God.*
- William Law

*What makes the ground Holy? What makes
a temple Holy? What makes anything Holy?
It is the claim to ownership by a Holy God.
We are not called to try to be holy. God's
claim on our lives makes us holy. But unlike
the ground, temple and other things we must
determine to remain Holy.*
- Ade Sobanjo

CHAPTER ONE

DETERMINE TO REMAIN HOLY

*..But as He who called you is holy, you also
be holy in all your conduct. (1 Peter 1:15
NKJV)*

It is important that right from the beginning of
your walk with God, you understand that you have been
called to holy living. God wants to make you holy. He
wants you to be committed to being holy and to trust
that he will make you holy. "Holy" here does not refer
only to an outward display of piety but rather to an all
encompassing realization that one belongs to God both
in thought and in action. It refers to a radical commitment to pleasing God in everything that we think or do.
It is only when you understand this that you can begin to
grow or develop as a Christian.

A holy life therefore will be filled with the love,
wisdom and the insight of God as well as lots more of
the virtues of God expressed in a unique way peculiar to
each individual. When you begin to see yourself as one
who is called to holy living, you begin to sense a greater
desire to know what God is doing and how He wants you

to be involved in His work. It is this desire that would now make you go to God in prayer for instructions as to what He would have you do.

As we take more time to let God speak to us and guide us; as we obey and yield to God's prompting, we become more and more like God. We recognize more of what God has made available to us through Jesus Christ, our lives become more fruitful and we bring more glory and joy to God our father. It is this process of transformation that is referred to as Christian growth. This growth is continuous and no one ever gets to a place that they are fully grown. The more we know God the more we grow. Take note that it is not the more we know about God but the more we know of God. The more intimate we become with Him. The more we learn to trust God and obey Him, the more we are said to be growing as Christians.

It is worthy of mention right from this first chapter that once you decide to let go of a self-centered lifestyle to pursue a God-centered one, you automatically trigger an active resistance from the enemy – the devil, the evil one, the tempter— whose sole aim is to oppose the purpose of God and as such to oppose you from having the joyful, peaceful and glorious life God has prepared for you. The enemy is the source of all the negative work that is being done on earth. It is through his deceit that humanity got enslaved in sin (a self-centered and ungodly life style). The ripple effect of our sins through several generations is the source of the pain and turmoil that we are experiencing today. Growth in Christ therefore, would involve a constant awareness that we are being opposed by the enemy and an increasing dependence on God to continually frustrate the attacks of the evil one.

The following chapters as mentioned earlier, discuss a few steps that every Christian should pay attention to - or emphasize in order to keep living a holy life and keep growing as a Christian. Growth is a natural characteristic of any living organism; so also as Christians, our spirits are fashioned to grow. However, just as there are things that can hamper natural growth such as disease, malnutrition, lack of rest and much more, there are also things that hamper our spiritual growth. My prayer is that as you read on, you will take note of a few steps that will help you keep your growth steady and on-track all through life's journey.

"The Lord wants all saved people to receive power from on High--power to witness, power to act, power to live, and power to show forth the divine manifestation of God within. The power of God will take you out of your own plans and put you into the plan of God. "
-Smith Wigglesworth

"How many Christians there are who cannot pray, and who seek by effort, resolve, joining prayer circles, etc., to cultivate in themselves the 'holy art of intercession,' and all to no purpose. Here for them and for all is the only secret of a real prayer life ---- 'Be filled with the Spirit,' who is 'the Spirit of grace and supplication.'"
-Rev. J. Stuart Holden

CHAPTER TWO

BE FILLED WITH THE HOLY SPIRIT

*Don't be drunk with wine, because that will
ruin your life. Instead, be filled with the
Holy Spirit. (Eph 5:18 NLT)*

Yes, the first step to Christian growth is to be filled with the Holy Spirit. I believe that as soon as one receives forgiveness of sins and begins a relationship with God, he must be filled with the Holy Spirit. For it is only one filled with the Holy Spirit who can fully enjoy the workings of the Holy Spirit in the life of a believer. Dear friend, you must endeavour to know as much as you can about the Holy Spirit and then ask Him to fill you. There are many fears and myths that have held a lot of people back from being filled with the Holy Spirit. However, these things are myths; they are not true and can only serve as hindrances to the will and purpose of God. Dear Christian, just as you have believed in Jesus for the redemption of your soul from eternal separation from God, you must also believe in Him as the baptizer with the Holy Spirit (Mark 1:8). Anyone who is totally surrendered to Christ, will find that they become filled with the Holy Spirit upon asking *(Luke 11:13)*.

The Bible teaches us that a person is composed of 3 parts as opposed to two which most of us are used to *(1 Thess 5:23, Heb 4:12)*. We are not simply mind and body; rather we are all made up of spirit, soul and body. The spirit is usually ignored or unnoticed because it is not being put to use, for it is through the spirit that we connect with God. Since many people are not in a continuous relationship with God, it is very easy to ignore or overlook the existence of the spirit. However, when we get born again or saved, what really happens is that we discover God's love through our spirits and as such our whole way of life is totally transformed. We suddenly are able to "see" the beauty of God's work on the cross and also the futility of all our human efforts. As a result of our spirits now being in contact with God, we are able to receive forgiveness and newness of life and God begins to mysteriously dwell in our spirits.

To be filled with the Holy Spirit therefore, is the next step after your spirit has been regenerated. You must allow the Holy Spirit to fill your heart with love. An individual filled with the Holy Spirit, becomes very conscious of the Holy Spirit and allows the Holy Spirit to guide him/her in this new walk with God and in this new life. It is only by the guidance of the Holy Spirit that any Christian can have any sustained growth in a relationship with God.

The Holy Spirit is always ready to fill any ready heart. As soon as we fulfill the required conditions, we are automatically filled. The conditions for being filled with the Holy Spirit are not strenuous. The first condition

is to desire to be filled with the Holy Spirit, to so desire
to be led of God that your spirit cries out to God for more
of God. Sometimes your mind may not understand your
desire, but your spirit yearns within you for communion
with God, for the direction from God, for the love of
God. Anyone who has such a desire is a sure candidate
for the filling with the Holy Spirit. The next condition is a
belief that the Holy Spirit has been given to anyone who
will receive Him. If you think that there is something
that you must do to deserve or merit the Holy Spirit's
infilling, you will be hindering yourself from receiving
it. As a believer, you must be assured that the Holy Spirit
is available to all who desire the Holy Spirit. No one can
ever merit the honour and blessing of an indwelling Holy
Spirit. It is a gift from God for which we must be eter-
nally grateful and willing to receive. Finally, you need to
ask to be filled and overwhelmed by the Holy Spirit as a
sign of your readiness to receive. Be assured that no one
is ever rejected of the Lord.

Here is a sample prayer to receive the infilling of
the Holy Spirit. –

Dear Father, I thank you for your promise
of your Holy Spirit. I thank you for the gift
of salvation. I am ready to serve you with all
of my life. I am ready to receive the fullness
of your spirit. I now receive the Holy Spirit.
Thank you for your love for me. Thank you
for filling me with your Holy Spirit. In Jesus
name I pray.

You may also speak with your small group leader or pastor to pray with you to receive the infilling of the Holy Spirit. Many people who received the Holy Spirit's infilling in biblical times had other Christians pray with them. It helps to strengthen your faith and encourage you to see others who love you and are also filled with the Holy Spirit. (Acts 8:14–17; Acts 19:6, Acts 9:17-19).

"Some people read their Bible in Hebrew, some in Greek; I like to read mine in the Holy Ghost."
- Smith Wigglesworth

"When filled with holy truth the mind rests."
— C.H. Spurgeon

CHAPTER THREE

BE FILLED WITH THE WORD OF GOD

But he answered, "It is written, 'Man does
not live by bread alone, but by every word
that comes from the mouth of God.'"
(Matthew 4:4 NET)

Something else I have discovered is that many new believers struggle to read the Bible. Some begin at Genesis and on getting to Leviticus, are about ready to give up. If you want to grow steadily as a Christian, you need to cultivate the habit of studying the Bible. It is not enough to just read it, but to really study to discover the treasures that are embedded in the scriptures. I find it quite helpful to use a study bible in a translation you find easy to understand. There are many guides that have been developed to help you read the entire bible, some of which can be found in study bibles.

Generally, I encourage new Christians to start reading the Bible from the New Testament; particularly the Gospel of John. This should be done with a view to learning as much as you can about Jesus. Once you are done reading the New Testament, you should also read the Old Testament. I find that reading with other people can make the exercise more fun and easier to complete.

You may choose to adopt a one-year or a three-year study plan to read the Bible. The focus however, is not on how long it takes you to complete the plan but on how much you gain from it and grow in the ability to hear a word for yourself from God. In other words, you must be able to learn something new that you can apply to your life every time you read the Bible. The things you learn everyday are the things that will continue to feed your spirit and make you more like Jesus.

Just like a natural baby is weak and helpless, so is a new Christian, weak and helpless without the word of God. It is very important that you realize that without a continuous study of the scriptures, you will remain weak and childish in your response to the spiritual challenges of life. It is easy to forget this truth in the midst of the excitement and the feeling of transformation that follows becoming a Christian but you must remember that your spirit needs to be fed regularly.

The word of God is the food of the human spirit. Jesus, when he was tempted by the devil in Matthew 4:4, said that a man must not live by bread alone, but by every word that proceeds from the mouth of God. In other words, Jesus is saying to us that the word of God is what our spirits live by. Just as it is important to feed our bodies daily, it is important for every Christian to read the bible daily. Many lives have been transformed by studying the Bible. Personally, I have found that the more I read the Bible prayerfully, the more I have gotten to know God, and trust Him. Sin becomes easier to re-sist when you are full of the word of God. The Psalmist says in Psalm 119:105 that "...thy word have I hid in my heart that I may not sin against thee". This highlights the importance of meditating on God's word. Meditation means to think about the portion of scripture that you have read asking yourself questions on how it can be applied to your life. You then take a note of whatever you have learned from the scripture in order to pray about it and refer to it again when you need to remember it.

As a new Christian, starting to read your Bible from the New Testament helps you get an understanding of the new covenant that brings us into a relationship with God through Jesus. You should make out time to read the Bible daily. You may start by spending a few minutes to read 10 to 15 verses a day or a chapter a day. I suggest that you don't read numerous chapters on one day and then go a week or two without reading the bible. No matter how many verses or chapters you read today, make it a habit to read some verses again tomorrow. Just like you don't eat a lot of food today and then not need to eat the next day, so also you should make effort to feed your spirit daily with a portion of scripture. Another analogy is the idea of building a relationship, it is always fun to read or hear from your loved one. If you want to grow in your relationship with God through Jesus, you need to read the word of God daily. The great evangelist Smith Wigglesworth was known to read a portion of the scriptures before every meal. He believed that it was more important to feed the spirit than the body, so before having any meal he took time to feed his spirit. It therefore comes as no surprise to read of the mighty works of miracle that occurred in his ministry.

The word of God builds your faith. The more you read the word of God, the more you know about the God of the word and the more you learn to trust Him. As you face different situations in life, the word of God in you will rise up and build faith in you to move mountains (that is, to surmount seemingly impossible challenges or difficulties). Therefore, I encourage you to take time out daily to study the word of God and determine within your heart to practice what you learn from it.

It is of no use reading the Bible if you have no intentions of obeying the instructions in it. Apostle James encourages us not to be hearers of the word only but doers also. Whenever you read the Bible, try to find out how the scripture applies to you today. Once you know how it applies to you, prayerfully adjust yourself to the word. Many Christians today are suffering and living below their maximum potential, not because of the devil's attack, or God's timing but because they are not spiritually healthy. They have been starving their spirits and so they have no spiritual stamina to do what they have been created and called to do.

Some portions of the Bible may be difficult to understand when reading them for the first time, especially when you do not have the benefit of knowing the contents of the other books or chapters of the Bible. This is why I usually encourage new believers to use a study Bible and be part of a bible study group. In this way, you can have answers to some of your questions. Nonetheless, if none of these resources are available to you, ask the Holy Spirit to reveal the meaning of the scripture to you and keep on reading. It is my experience, that as I have read the scriptures over the years, I have come to have a deeper understanding of some of the scriptures to which I lacked understanding earlier in my spiritual walk with God.

Before going on with this booklet, make a note of what time you will set aside for studying the bible daily. Also find out when you can attend a bible study at your church. Decide to join this group every week. This is a very important part of your life so make whatever changes are necessary to ensure that you attend a Bible study weekly. Some church families have small groups that meet in homes on different days and time. Find one of these home groups and become actively involved in it.

My Daily Bible Study Plan:

When_____

Where_____

"Worship renews the spirit as sleep renews the body."
- Richard Clarke Cabot

"Have you noticed how much praying for revival has been going on of late - and how little revival has resulted? I believe the problem is that we have been trying to substitute praying for obeying, and it simply will not work. To pray for revival while ignoring the plain precept laid down in Scripture is to waste a lot of words and get nothing for our trouble. Prayer will become effective when we stop using it as a substitute for obedience." - A. W. Tozer

Whatever you can think about, you can pray about. As soon as I realized that God knows my thoughts, I also understood that there is no topic that I cannot talk to God about.
- Ade Sobanjo

Is prayer your steering wheel or your spare tire?-- Corrie Ten Boom

CHAPTER FOUR

PRAY ALWAYS 24-7

Never stop praying.
(1Thess 5:17 NLT)

Prayer can simply be described as communing with God. You can pray at anytime; even when you sin or fail in life. The best thing to do when we find that we have sinned is actually to pray. Talk to God; ask for mercy and grace never to repeat the sin. Although we may feel or think that we have disappointed God at this time, God is aware of the sin and He is always available to help us overcome the weaknesses and lack of knowledge that cause us to sin. With time, you will notice that praying always empowers you to overcome many of the sinful tendencies in your life.

Prayer is the only way to bring the power of God down into our lives. Just as it is important that a child communicate with his parents, so it is important for us to speak to God our heavenly father. You should talk to God about your daily activities, ask him to empower you to obey his words as you read them daily, ask him to help you draw closer to him. Whatever you can think about, you can pray about. As soon as I realized that

God knows my thoughts, I also understood that there is no topic that I cannot talk to God about. It is important to understand that prayer can be described as allowing God to influence or intervene in your life. By praying about your thoughts, your fears, your failures, your successes, your questions and so on, you are simply allowing God to be involved in bringing His positive and glorious influence into the situation.

Prayer is sometimes a mystery to new Christians. They wonder if they have to assume some specific posture, or say some specific words or follow certain rituals. Prayer is not supposed to be such a mystery. Prayer is as easy as speaking to your friend. The weakest person on earth can pray, the strongest person can pray, the new Christian can pray and the matured Christian can pray.

I suggest that you make out time to pray after reading your bible. For example, if you plan on reading a few verses every day, then take out an extra 10 minutes to pray after studying the Bible. It is advisable to prepare a list of things to pray about before going to God in prayers. Making a list, helps you to stay focused and to cover a lot of ground within the period you have. Many Christians have complained that they do not know how to pray for long periods of time. They wonder how older Christians can spend two to three hours in prayers. My suggestion is that you keep a little diary with you all day and in that diary write down things you would like to present to your father, God during your next prayer time. You will notice that as you begin to make a habit of noting things to pray about, you will actually spend more time in prayer. Having a list of things to pray about also helps you know when the answers to your prayers become manifested. You will be able to go over your list to tick or cross off those prayer points to which you have seen the answers.

It is good practice that you learn to start your time of prayer with a session of praise and thanksgiving. Spend the first few minutes to praise God for whom He is: a great loving father, ever faithful, ever loving and merciful. Praise God for all the great attributes that you have learnt about Him as you have been reading the bible and then spend some more time to thank the Lord for the things he has done for you. A good way to do this will be to spend some time to think about the things that God has done for you. Thank Him for the gift of life, health, salvation, family, love, employment (if you are employed), shelter etc. It is important that you never forget the love and blessings of God. In my life, I have discovered that every time I spend time praising and thanking God, His presence comes down and I become very much inspired to pray and spiritually empowered. The psalmist explains this by declaring that God is enthroned on the praises of Israel (Psalm 22:3). In other words, God enjoys and desires the praises of His people. Another way of looking at it is that wherever God is being praised, God is very much present there and He is not just present but ready to manifest Himself. God is everywhere, but God does not manifest His presence everywhere. Where God ALWAYS manifests His presence however, is in the praises of His people.

After spending time to praise and thank God, you may then present yourself to God. Tell God that you are willing to obey Him and that you want Him to guide you through the rest of the day. If any sins come to mind, don't feel guilty and stop praying. The devil has deceived many young Christians in this manner. If any sins come to mind, immediately ask for forgiveness; determine in your heart not to repeat the sin, ask God to help you not to return to it, and then go on in your prayers. Once you ask God to forgive you with a sincere heart and decide never to return to that sin, God forgives you. You can then go ahead and present your list to God. If you follow the model that I have suggested above, you will discover that you can spend at least 15 mins in prayers. As you practice the habit of praying daily, you will discover that your prayer list is getting longer and you are spending more time in prayer.

Remember to ask God to guide you throughout the day. As a Christian, you belong to God and it is only reasonable to ask God to tell you what He wants to do in the different situations that you face daily. God will guide you by giving you ideas and impressions in your spirit about what he wants you to do or not to do. As you get these impressions, it is important that you learn to follow them. These impressions are referred to by some people as intuition. You just find that you "feel" or sort of know that you should or should not be doing something or the other. As we learn to follow the leading of the Holy Spirit in our hearts, we start to learn to recognize His voice. It is important however, to note that the Holy

Spirit will not guide you against the revealed will of God as stated in the Bible.

It is always my suggestion that once a Christian is saved he/she should immediately begin to desire to be filled with the Holy Spirit. Once filled, begin to spend some time praying in the spirit or praying in other tongues as the Holy Spirit gives you utterance. When we spend time in the place of prayer and we pray in tongues, our spirits communicate with God and we are edified. I have discovered over the years that as I spend time to pray in the spirit, that I am so much more aware of God's love and my faith seems to increase.

"Has it ever occurred to you that one hundred pianos all tuned to the same fork are automatically tuned to each other? They are of one accord by being tuned, not to each other, but to another standard to which each one must individually bow. So one hundred worshippers meeting together, each one looking away to Christ, are in heart nearer to each other than they could possibly be were they to become 'unity' conscious and turn their eyes away from God to strive for closer fellowship. Social religion is perfected when private religion is purified. The body becomes stronger as its members become healthier. The whole church of God gains when the members that compose it begin to seek a better and a higher life."
— A. W. Tozer

CHAPTER FIVE

BE PART OF A CHURCH FAMILY

*Let us not give up meeting together, as some
are in the habit of doing, but let us encourage one another--and all the more as you
see the Day approaching.
(Heb 10:25 NIV)*

One of the instructions we give to new believers
that come to Jesus outside the cities where our churches
are located is this: "Attend a church where Christ is hon-
oured, the Bible is taught and everyone is welcomed." It
is important that you begin to attend church regularly. If
you intend to grow spiritually, you need to invest some
time in developing your spirit. Do not attend church on
Sundays alone. Attend a Bible Study meeting at your
church and the prayer meeting. A rule of thumb for the
number of times to attend church meetings for a growing
Christian is three times.

It is true that going to church does not automatically translate into growth. However, for a Christian
that is already growing, attending the Bible study or a
small group meeting at church would help you to grow
faster and become more balanced. This is as a result of
the opportunity it gives you to share some of the things

that you are learning at your personal Bible study time and also to ask questions about the challenges that you face as a growing Christian. The Spirit of the Lord encourages us not to abandon the gathering together of the Christian brothers and sisters. Personally, I enjoyed a balanced spiritual growth because when I began growing as a Christian, I had the great privilege of attending a university campus fellowship where I had the opportunity of meeting many Christians who were much more spiritually matured than myself and I could look up to them and aspire to develop the Christ-like characteristics I saw in them. I had a Christian fellowship meeting almost every day and sometimes twice daily. In addition to these, I took time to pray with a few friends and I prayed and studied the Bible on my own too. One major mistake that we Christians make is substituting church meetings for our personal time with God. NEVER DO THAT. No matter how much time you spend fellowshipping with the children of God, it is still important that you take time to meet with God alone. It is during this time alone with God that you digest and reflect on what you are learning; you can then personally own some of these lessons.

I have been shocked by many Christians in my few years in ministry. I have seen brothers and sisters that have been very active in church and whom we would assume have a solid foundation in their personal walk, do unimaginable things when left alone. Many have committed all sorts of sins because they did not learn to develop themselves alone with God, while they were getting involved in the church meetings. So use the time you spend with other believers to enrich your time alone with God. Let the fellowship with others inspire a desire to spend more time alone with God so that you can also know God the way your spiritual leaders and other more matured believers know Him.

I remember that when I used to see other believers praying for one or more hours; it made me want to know God more, to learn how to spend more time with God. Also when I heard how other people explained the truths in the Bible, it made me want to spend more time studying scriptures so that I could know all the resources that are available to me as a believer. Fellowshipping with others also builds our faith because we get the opportunity to hear the experiences of others and how God is faithful to them. Their stories help us see that we can also grow and do what they are doing. These testimonies help us to believe that if God did it for John or Jane He can and would do it for me and in me also.

Finally, being involved in church meetings and small groups helps in developing our skills as leaders in the community, and in developing love for the people of God. It also enables us to work with others and to share the love of God that we experience with them.

Dear Christian, whenever you begin to sense a need to be alone and not attend Christian meetings anymore, let it be a sign that something is not right with your walk with God. Don't get me wrong. I know there are times when we need to get away from the crowd to be alone with God, to enjoy our Lord and Saviour without the noise and distractions from any other person. When this occurs, it is usually for relatively short periods of time – say 3 days, a week or on rare occasions, a couple of weeks at a stretch. The time spent on a retreat and being alone with God, leaves you looking forward to the time you will be back with the people of God and sharing His love them. If on the contrary, you begin to discover that you do not want to go to church services or small group meetings, please check your heart to identify the source of such feelings. It is not unusual at this time to find that you are not enjoying your personal time of prayer and Bible study as well.

CHAPTER SIX

SHARE THE GOOD NEWS

*The woman then left her waterpot, went
her way into the city, and said to the men,
"Come, see a Man who told me all things
that I ever did. Could this be the Christ?"
Then they went out of the city and came to
Him.
(John 4:28-30 NKJV)*

    I have never had to tell a new Christian to share
the good news of their salvation. The joy and the peace
that springs up from within is usually too much to keep
silent about. Making a commitment to Christ is a won-
derful thing indeed. It is the most important decision you
would ever make. Your life stops being focused and centered on yourself and becomes rather, centered and focused on God through Jesus Christ. As soon as you make
this decision, you will notice a change in your life. Many
notice an amazing amount of peace and joy; others, a
new perspective to life. It has been described as feeling
like saying hello to everyone you meet, the flowers look
brighter, and even the winter is not as depressing. However, this sudden change may confuse your family and

friends who are non-Christians. They may assume that they are loosing your attention and participation in their lives. Consequently, they might respond to your news with hostility as has been the experience of many others. My suggestion therefore, is that you share your new commitment with friends and family beginning with those that would be happy to hear about it. The next step would be to plan to share the good news of your new found relationship with someone new on a regular basis. Many Christians after sharing their testimonies with people that are hostile become very shy and afraid to continue sharing their testimonies. This is why I encourage new Christians to begin sharing their faith with people who would be excited to hear it first before going on to share with those who may not understand what is happening and may want to "protect" you from it.

Sharing the good news with others, does not require you to know so many scriptures or to prepare a sermon. All you have to do is tell the other person your story. However, I would suggest that you prepare the story before going ahead to share it. Write your story on a sheet of paper and read it to yourself. Make sure it is coherent and would make sense to a non-Christian. If you are new to Christianity, not having grown up around Christian "lingo", your testimony would be easy to understand. Interestingly, I have found that many people get more people saved in their first few weeks of becoming Christians than some who have been Christians for many years. It is important therefore, that you begin to share your testimony as soon as possible so you can cultivate the habit of sharing the good news right from the onset of your Christian growth.

Over and over again in the ministry of Jesus, he made it clear that his mission was to set sinners free from their sins (Mark 2:17, John 4:34-36, Luke 4:18). As soon as Christ begins to reign in our hearts by His Spirit, we are drawn into this honourable work of sharing the love of God and the good news of God's Kingdom with those who are not yet a part of it. Before leaving the earth, in His final speech to his disciples, Jesus commands them to go into all the world and make disciples. Once you become a disciple of Jesus, you should immediately start to help in the process of making more disciples.

Sharing the love of God (Jesus) with others is not as difficult as it sounds. Remembering how you wish someone had told you earlier about Christ, should motivate you to share Him with others. I encourage you to cultivate the habit of making friends all around you and then seize every opportunity presented to you to tell the story of what Jesus has done in your life. In my Christian walk so far, I have come to learn that as long as I am ready to share my story, opportunities to do so always arise. God then takes what you share as the tool with which He draws others to himself.

*"Tell me what you do with your time and money
and I will tell you where your heart is."*
- Xavier

*"No one has the right to hear the gospel twice,
while there remains someone who has not heard
it once." -- Oswald J. Smith*

CHAPTER SEVEN

OFFER YOUR TIME, MONEY AND TALENTS TO THE SERVICE OF CHRIST.

So let each one give as he purposes in his heart, not grudgingly or of necessity; for God loves a cheerful giver. And God is able to make all grace abound toward you, that you, always having all sufficiency in all things, may have an abundance for every good work.
(2 Corinthians 9:7-8 NKJV)

It is important that as soon as you begin a relationship with God through Christ, that you begin to give regularly to the things of God. Start by volunteering at the church service. Help with the setting-up of the church; caring for the little children or during special programs. If you have a very busy schedule and are unable to spare the time, give money to the church instead. Your money is the result of your labour so if you give money it is like giving your time. It is recommended however, that every Christian that intends to grow spiritually give a minimum of 10% of their income to the work of God (Mal 3;10-12). This is known as tithing. In the old covenant, it was mandatory for the people of God to bring 10% of their increase to the temple, to support the Levites and the upkeep of the temple. In the same way, it is necessary that Christians today give at least 10% of their income towards the work and mission of Christ in the church. For example, if you earn $2000 a month, you should give at least $200. When you do this, you will discover the joy of giving and also the blessing that comes from giving to the work of God. Doors of increase will be opened to you and your finances will be protected by God. I have noticed over the years that when I paid my tithes, I was able to do more with what was left than when I spent all the money on my own stuff. The habit of giving to the Lord blesses the giver more than it blesses the church.

Please do not fall into the error of thinking that you can only give when you have a lot of money. Even if you are on welfare and you receive only $300 a month. I recommend that you still give $30 to the work of God. The way I went about it when I was really broke was that if 90% of the money could not meet my needs anyway, 100% wouldn't help either. I have given tithes of $5 when I had only $50. It is important to start giving when you have little so that it becomes a habit and as God blesses you and you have plenty it would not be hard to give your tithes. I would let you into a secret: the best way to help your giving habit is to realize that when you give your life to Christ, you give him your finances too, 100% of the money belongs to God anyway. He is your true source of income. Your job, friends, business, grants, bursaries and so on are simply avenues that God uses to provide for you.

In the Bible, we are encouraged to give more than the tithe (10%) of our increase. In the early church, people sold their houses, lands and other properties to give towards the work of ministry. I remember when I was trying to understand the concept of tips in the restaurants in Canada. I had to ask what the recommended amount to give as tips was and I was told about 15%. Similarly, I believe the minimum amount that we are to give to the work of God is 10% but we are encouraged to give more, to give our time, to use our skills and to do all that is within our power to promote the work of the kingdom of God.

Many Christians find it really difficult to give 10% of their income to the work of spreading the love of God to others. This is simply because they have lost their appreciation for the love of Christ which they received. They now place more value on the money they are earning than on the work to which they have been called. Anyone who claims to be living for God will not find it difficult to commit at least 10% of their time, talent and other resources to the work of God. Give your tithe to the local church group where you are being developed spiritually and serving. You want that ministry to continue to be a blessing to many others.

Giving involves more than giving money. It also involves giving your talents, connections, time and any other resources that you may have been blessed with. Giving is a good way of expressing your love to God. Please do not think that giving lots of money to the work of God would replace, spending time alone with God in prayers, studying the bible or sharing the good news about your relationship with Christ. Giving is just one of the habits that help to develop a balanced and healthy relationship with the Lord. I assure you that if you are faithful to these habits; if you are consistent and refuse to give up even when you fail, you will discover that you would develop a strong robust relationship with the Lord. You will find that you have joy unspeakable, peace that is beyond understanding, faith to face life's problems and lots of love to spread around as you participate in bringing the love of God to the world.

CHAPTER EIGHT

REMEMBER THAT YOU HAVE AN ENEMY

*Be alert and of sober mind. Your enemy
the devil prowls around like a roaring lion
looking for someone to devour. Resist him,
standing firm in the faith, because you know
that the family of believers throughout the
world is undergoing the same kind of suffer-
ings.*
(1 Pet 5:8 NIV)

The most difficult enemy to combat is the one
that you are unaware of. If you have an unknown enemy,
you are virtually at the mercy of such an enemy because
he can pretend to be your friend and do you great harm.
This is why we are reminded in the scripture above to be
alert. Every human being has an enemy. The Bible calls
this enemy several names in line with his activities – he
is called the devil, the accuser, the thief, Satan.

When we choose to live our lives for Christ; our
enemy, the devil intensifies his activities to discourage
us and to try to get us to return to our former lives of
bondage to sin under his control. As a new believer, this
period can be very confusing because you assume that as
soon as you give your life to Christ, all temptations will

cease and you will have breakthroughs all around.

It is true that when we receive the life of Christ, all things are made new and we have access to God our father and his authority to overcome the works of the devil. However, our enemy, the devil continually tries to stop us by bombarding us with a series of trials and temptations. At this time, it is important for you to know that being a child of God does not protect you from being tempted. Jesus was tempted and all his disciples in the scriptures were also tempted. Temptation is not sin; it is simply an attempt of the enemy to draw us into sin. As a child of God therefore, you must resist the devil, continually choosing to say no to the temptations of the enemy and sharing your challenges with other Christians who are close to you, particularly your small group leader. As you learn to resist the devil, you will discover that the temptations become relatively less intense in the areas in which you are learning to trust Christ as your strength. This process will continue all through your Christian walk because temptations serve to remind us of our need to call on Christ to help with each temptation.

Please be reminded, that it is Christ in you that makes the difference. Forgetting this truth and trying to resist temptations in your strength, would only result in failure. For every temptation or trial (negative situation), the new Christian must draw strength from the Christ who dwells in him by His Spirit. Apart from temptations, many new Christians have also experienced persecutions (negative reactions from friends, neighbours, colleagues etc) and trials. For example, a new Christian may lose his job, lock her keys in the car, fall down during the winter and many such inconveniences. Please do not allow any of these inconveniences distract you. Rather, let them push you to the place of prayer. Remember that they are designed by your enemy to take your eyes off your Lord and Saviour, Jesus and focus them on the situations around you. Decide from now on that no matter what happens, you will call on the Lord for help rather than panic and get discouraged.

As you grow in your faith in God, you will learn to fill your thoughts with prayers and these attempts of the enemy to distract you will always meet with the wisdom and comfort from the Spirit of God. You will soon realize that God allows some of these things to help you move forward in your walk with him.

Finally, I would like to encourage you to take the authority you have as a child of God and reject any thing that you see in your life or around you that you know in your heart is not from God. Learn to say no to these works of the enemy in the name of Jesus. For instance, if you discover that you are always falling ill, say I reject {mention the name of the sickness} in my life in Jesus Name. Make a habit of always rejecting anything you believe Jesus will reject and permit only the things you believe Jesus will permit. At first, this exercise may seem strange, but as you develop your relationship with God you will notice that when you take sides with God on issues, they become real as opposed to when you accept only what you can understand from your physical senses.

When Jesus was on earth, He always challenged the works of the enemy. When he saw someone blind, he simply said to the blind man – open your eyes, or go and wash your eyes in the river after rubbing some mud on it. He told a man with a withered hand to stretch out his arm. We also, must challenge the work of the enemy in our lives. If you are having a bad day, people are being mean to you, and everything seems to be going wrong, instead of getting upset, simply begin to declare the word of God concerning the situation. You may say something like this:

In the name of Jesus, I choose to have a good day. I take charge over the situations around me. I receive wisdom right now and patience. Holy Spirit, help me and guide me. I receive peace all around me right now in Jesus Name. Devil, take your hands off my day, my car...

The more you do this, the more you will walk in your place as a child of the Almighty God. You are a child of the King of kings. You have the Spirit of the Almighty God in you. Don't settle for less than what God has bought for you through Christ on the cross.

CONCLUSION

Growing in your Christian faith is a lifelong journey. What we have received from God is so vast that it
would take a lifetime and all of eternity to fully discover
it all. No one ever comes to a point in their faith when
they are no longer growing. If you ever come across a
Christian that says that "I don't think I need to read the
Bible anymore because I have read it all and I know
everything in it"; or a Christian that no longer feels the
need to pray, be assured that you have met a backslidden
Christian. We are to continuously draw nearer to God
and grow unto maturity.

You must ensure that you are always growing.
It is not the number of hours that you spend that counts,
but rather the quality of what is being done. It is better to spend 5mins in a quiet location with a note book
studying the word, than spend 20min on the bus studying
the Bible while being distracted all around. Also, strive
to continuously improve the quality and amount of time
you spend on the steps discussed in this booklet. For, if
you give yourself to these things, you would be glad you
did.

As you study the word of God and pray, the Holy
Spirit will guide you into other things that would help
you become the person he made you to be. You would
learn how to: pray more, receive your miracles, resist
the enemy, be filled with the Holy Spirit, manifest the
gifts of the spirit, release the love of God that is in you

and discover your ministry gifts. Dear friend, let us go deeper, let us develop our love relationship with God, let us work with the Holy Spirit to bring the Kingdom of God here on earth.

This booklet was not written as an exhaustive treatise on the Christian life. My goal in writing it is to help new Christians start off their Christian walk on a good foundation. It is an answer to the questions asked by visitors to our church meetings over the years. If you are a growing Christian, you may find this booklet useful as a tool to help others or simply to remind yourself of the basics of your faith. You may discover that I have not treated any of the topics deeply; this is intentional as I want this book to be an easy read. A book that can be read in a day or two and referred to often during early Christian growth. This booklet can also be used by follow-up counsellors to instruct new converts. However, to do a discipleship program, you would need a more detailed and interactive book.

If this booklet has been a blessing to you, please let me know at ade@adesobanjo.com.

www.ingramcontent.com/pod-product-compliance
Lightning Source LLC
Chambersburg PA
CBHW060541030426
42337CB00021B/4369